P9-DHP-016

The New York Times

POCKET
MBA
SERIES

SALES & MARKETING
25 KEYS TO SELLING YOUR PRODUCTS

MICHAEL A. KAMINS, PH.D.
Marshall School of Business Administration
University of Southern California

LF

Lebhar-Friedman Books
NEW YORK • CHICAGO • LOS ANGELES • LONDON • PARIS • TOKYO

For *The New York Times*
Mike Levitas, Editorial Director, Book Development
Tom Redburn, General Series Editor
Brent Bowers, Series Editor
James Schembari, Series Editor

Lebhar-Friedman Books
425 Park Avenue
New York, NY 10022

Published by Lebhar-Friedman Books
Lebhar-Friedman Books is a company of Lebhar-Friedman Inc.

Printed in the United States of America

Library of Congress Cataloging-in-Publication Data
Kamins, Michael A.
    Sales & marketing : 25 keys to selling your products /
Michael A. Kamins.
        p.   cm.—(The New York Times pocket MBA series ; vol. 8)
    Includes index.
    ISBN 0-86730-773-0 (pbk.)
    1. Selling.   2. Marketing.   3. Sales management.
4. Advertising   I. Title.   II. Title: Sales & marketing   III. Series.
    HF5438.25 .K346   1999
    658.8—dc21   99-27702
                                                        CIP

DESIGN & PRODUCTION BY MILLER WILLIAMS DESIGN ASSOCIATES

Visit our Web site at lfbooks.com

INTRODUCTION

LEBHAR-FRIEDMAN BOOKS is proud to present *The New York Times* Pocket MBA Series, 12 invaluable reference volumes that are easily accessible to all businesspersons, from first level managers to the executive suite. The books are written by Ph.D.s who teach in the MBA programs in some of the finest schools in the country. A team of business editors from *The New York Times*— Mike Levitas, Tom Redburn, Brent Bowers, and James Schembari—provided their own expertise to edit a reference series that is beyond compare.

The New York Times Pocket MBA Series offers quick-reference key points learned in top MBA programs. The 25-key structure of each volume presents an unparalleled synopsis of crucial principles of specific areas of business expertise. The unique approach to this series packages academic books for consumers in an easy-to-use trade format that is ideal for the individual businessperson as well as an excellent training reference manual. Be sure to get all 12 titles in the series to complete your own MBA education.

Joseph Mills
Senior Managing Editor
Lebhar-Friedman Books

The New York Times Pocket MBA
Series includes these 12 volumes:

Analyzing Financial Statements

Business Planning

Business Financing

Growing & Managing a Business

Organizing a Company

Forecasting Budgets

Tracking & Controlling Costs

Sales & Marketing

Managing Investment

Going Global

Leadership & Vision

The Board of Directors

25 KEYS TO SELLING YOUR PRODUCTS

CONTENTS

The need to understand the complexity of marketing

I've been to many dinner parties where people ask me what I do for a living. I used to say, "I practice and teach marketing." The typical response would be: "Oh . . . so you're the guy who creates the need for a product I don't really want," or "Marketing is just selling, and selling is something most everyone knows how to do." After spending most of my time at parties correcting these misperceptions, I now have decided to reposition myself at future events as a Professor of Advanced Marketing Research and Quantitative Methods. This, of course, will kill any form of dinner conversation, but should do wonders for the thinking time I need to write this book, which I plan to hand to guests at future events when I again describe myself as a marketing academic and practitioner. So two questions come to the forefront: 1) What is marketing? and 2) How does it differ from selling?

MARKETING IS NOT JUST SELLING. IT IS *STRATEGY*
Marketing has been defined by the American

Marketing Association as, "The process of planning and executing the conception, pricing, promotion, and distribution of ideas, goods and services to create exchanges that satisfy individual and organizational objectives."

This is a rather complex definition, and it suggests that the marketing process is not being practiced by the used car salesman at the auto mall who says "Pssst, come over here, I've got the exact car you want at the price you can afford." The fact that he has never met you before in his life is of little consequence.

He is trying to sell you the product and not market the product to you.

Selling, and marketing are quite different. For one, as Levitt (1960) points out in his classic article titled "Marketing Myopia," there are many differences between marketing and selling. Selling focuses on the needs of the seller, marketing on the needs of the buyer. The focus of selling is on the need of manufacturers to turn their product into cash while the focus of marketing ultimately is consumer satisfaction, which is derived from an in-depth knowledge of the consumer's needs and wants as well as a carefully thought out marketing strategy. That is, the product, its price, promotion and distribution must be considered when meeting the needs of the customer.

MARKETING'S 4 P'S: THE "MARKETING MIX"

The marketing process and, hence, marketing strategy is integrated and rather complex. It essentially involves two distinct components. The first component is the "Marketing Mix," a term coined by James Culliton and made popular by an article written by Neal Borden in 1964. According to Culliton, the marketing manager is a "mixer of ingredients," inclusive of product, price, promotion and distribution. That is, the marketing manager and the firm can strategically adapt these components in the construction of the final product. For example, Saturn has chosen to price their car rather inexpensively, has promoted the car mainly through television advertisements and billboards and distributes the car exclusively through Saturn dealerships. The car as a product is well known for its safety features and for its innovation, hence the celestial name Saturn (e.g., this year they introduced the world's first 3-door sports car).

Saturn's strategy cannot be evaluated regarding its' effectiveness unless it is known who they are selling to. That is, who is their target market? This is the second component of marketing strategy.

DEFINING THE TARGET MARKET

It should be obvious that the marketing mix cannot be developed independent of the target market. No matter how creative the marketing mix, it cannot stand alone. For example, if Saturn declared that their target market was current Mercedes owners, their strategy would be relatively ineffective. For starters, Mercedes owners are looking for a luxury car, which a Saturn is not. Saturn typically focuses on a younger market who are looking for a first car and who are both price and safety conscious. Hence their target market fits their marketing mix. This is the essence of good marketing: design a marketing mix that fits an identified target market. A mis-match between target market and marketing mix can be the cause of product failure. For example, the introduction of a product called "sweat" used in Japan to replenish thirst after heavy exercise would be problematic in America where drinking something of that name would be less than desirable for any target market. Likewise, Ford's new gigantic sports utility vehicle "The Excursion," positioned to sell to current S.U.V. owners, may take its last excursion if the target market finds issue with components of the truck, such as width (need for two parking spaces) and height (difficult to enter the car and various parking structures).

Developing the correct marketing mix for the appropriate target market is a prerequisite for effective marketing strategy. Next comes positioning.

Positioning and why it is important in guiding marketing strategy

---

Recently, I was in a rush to get to the East Coast from Los Angeles. I called a local airline and asked if they had a "red-eye" available that very night to fly to New York. I was told that "we do not have red-eyes, sir." I responded, "You mean to tell me that you have no night flights to New York? I find that hard to believe."

The reservation agent replied, "I never said we have no night flights, I just said that we have no red-eyes. It so happens that we have a wonderful flight called the *Moonlight Special* leaving Los Angeles at 11:00 this evening, connecting in Houston and arriving in New York about 11:00 the next morning." I quickly said: "Please book me on that red-eye."

It seems obvious to me that most consumers, if given the choice, would rather fly the "moonlight special" than the "red-eye," even though they are exactly the same thing. The lesson is that the consumer's response to the product or service is

The concerns that are most successful are those that know most about their prospective customers.

Roger Babson, **Business Fundamentals**

linked to the way they are positioned. But what is positioning? According to Kotler (1994, p.307), it is "the act of designing the company's offer and image so that it occupies a distinct and valued place in the target customers' mind." Ries and Trout (1993) argue that it is the place that the product occupies in the consumer's mind. Hence, Volvo is positioned as the safe automobile, *Investor's Business Daily* is positioned as the Wall Street newspaper that makes you money, and Lucky is positioned as the low-price supermarket.

THE UNIQUE SELLING PROPOSITION (U.S.P.)
The U.S.P. is a unique product attribute that a company uses to set its brand apart from the competition. For example, a big food company was the first to emphasize that its tuna was "Dolphin Safe." Folger's is the only coffee that focuses on

the fact that it is mountain grown (although one should realize that little coffee is grown in Kansas and Nebraska). We all know that Avis tries harder.

Emphasizing a single attribute as a tactic to position your brand can be advantageous in that it allows you to focus all of your marketing efforts on that one attribute. However, it can also be a dangerous strategy because it must be identified as an attribute that your target market values as important. In addition, because you are hanging your hat on one attribute to position your brand, the competition may have an easier time to attack you.

First, they can try to downplay the importance of the attribute you are emphasizing. For example, at one point Lowenbrau stated they were the best-selling German beer in America, but Beck's countered by stating they were the best-selling German beer in Germany. So the question was whether one would rather drink the German beer most popular in Germany or the German beer most popular in America. I think we all know the answer to this one.

The competition can also introduce an attribute that makes your attribute obsolete. For example, Ultrabrite positioned itself on the brightening of teeth. However that positioning became eclipsed when toothpaste specifically invented for hardcore tooth whitening came to market (e.g., Rembrandt and Pearl Drops).

A SLOGAN IS BETTER THAN 1,000 WORDS
Can you identify the comedian who says:

"I don't get no respect."

"Can we talk?"

"Thanks for the memories."

The answers should be obvious: Rodney Dangerfield, Joan Rivers, and Bob Hope. In a way, this short sentence sets each comedian apart and gives the listener a piece of information about what the comedian is all about. What works in comedy works in marketing.

When George Zimmer of the Men's Warehouse says "I guarantee it," he stands apart from the rest in terms of conveying his U.S.P. that you can trust his company's quality and service. When Larry Miller of Sit 'n' Sleep screams: "I'll meet anyone's advertised price or your mattress is freeeeeee. . . ," he is conveying the message that his store charges less than the competition and one shouldn't shop elsewhere.

Consistency is the key when it comes to slogans. It should be consistent with the intended positioning of the brand and in general it should be consistent over time. When the marketing climate changes the company's positioning, the slogan should also. For example, Kaiser Permanente, a health maintenance organization, recently changed its slogan to "In the Hands of Doctors," which effectively addresses the recent attack on managed care suggesting that insurance companies and hospital administration have become the gatekeepers of care.

KEY 3

Why the job of the marketing manager is key to the success of the firm

W hat does a marketing manager do? In a nutshell the job of the marketing manager is to monitor and attempt to regulate demand thorough the adaptation of the marketing mix (the 4 P's) to the target market. The marketing manager makes the crucial marketing decisions in the company. Like all management positions, marketing management involves the analysis, planning, implementation and monitoring or control of marketing programs designed to achieve company objectives.

Here's an example. Suppose that you are the marketing manager of a large and famous toy company whose profit and revenues are closely tied to a popular doll (let's call her Lindsey), which mainly appeals to young girls between the ages of 6–12. Additionally, assume that in the eyes of the target market this doll is perceived to be of college age, trendy in fashion, and bubbly in personality.

Your major competitor has determined that they

can gain a foothold in the doll market by introducing a doll (Jane) that is similar in all respects to your doll only that it is positioned as being of high-school age. What do you do? Do you let the competition pioneer this potentially lucrative and untouched market by doing nothing? Do you attack the competition, and if so, how? These are issues that the marketing manager must deal with in the creation of a battle plan to maintain market share for a doll that is critical to the success of your company.

What actually happened is that this large and famous toy company challenged the competition through the introduction of a doll (Linda), who was positioned as the younger cousin of Lindsey. This was a brilliant marketing decision by the marketing manager, as young girls asked themselves, would I rather play with Linda, who is the cousin of the well-known Lindsey, or with Jane who in all respects is just simply plain? The answer to this question is obvious. The end result is that Lindsey and Linda won the marketing battle and the company now owns the high-school age doll market.

What is left for the competitor to do after the battle has been lost? Their marketing manager has engineered a strategy that involves the creation of dolls for young girls modeled after famous celebrity singers. After all, it would be hard to claim that Lindsey or Linda is related to Madonna and even more questionable to claim a family relationship to Marilyn Manson.

The doll wars continue.

POSITIONING THE PRODUCT TO THE APPROPRIATE TARGET MARKET

Any marketing program will be ineffective if it is

not positioned to the correct target market. It is the marketing manager's job to insure that the appropriate target market has been identified. For example, in 1979 when the decision to introduce Absolut Vodka into the United States was in the process of being made, Michel Roux (director of marketing at Carrillon Importers) positioned the brand as a status symbol through higher pricing and a distinctively shaped bottle. He described his target market as appropriately "the upper end, trend-setting, artsy crowd." No one can argue with the brand's success as it became the top-selling imported vodka in the United States just five years after introduction.

The identification of the appropriate target market for a brand is not simple and involves extensive marketing research, which will be covered in Key 6. The worst mistake that a marketing manager can make is to identify a target market through gut feeling rather than hard empirical data.

KEY 4

Understanding why knowledge of the marketing environment contributes to a firm's success

In Key 1, we discussed the marketing mix (or 4 P's) and the target market as critical elements of marketing strategy. If the reader could visualize a bulls-eye with the target market at the center, the 4 P's would represent the first ring surrounding the bulls-eye. Importantly, the 4 P's are under the control of the marketing manager to a large degree as price is set by the firm, as are product specifications, the promotional budget and the distribution plan.

The marketing environment, which represents the second ring around the bulls-eye, is not under the marketing manager's control and represents the conditions under which the marketing strategy is implemented. It is these conditions that must continuously be monitored and attended to by the marketing manager. Failure to keep a pulse on changes in the marketing environment can rapidly lead to the demise of a marketing strategy that had previously been successful. What follows is a discussion of each of the marketing environments:

The Social and Cultural Environment

When introducing a product, the marketer should study social customs and cultural mores. For example, many believed that McDonald's would not be a great success in France because the French typically dined on five-course meals lasting for over an hour with wine as a staple. How was a fast-food experience to survive? It was simple. When outside tables were added and wine was served, McDonald's became a viable lunch option for those workers who typically were given less than an hour to eat!

Sometimes it takes a sensitivity to the subculture in one's own country to be an effective marketer. For example, the Anaheim Angels serve kosher hot dogs appealing to the Jewish community, whereas the Dodgers have many Jewish fans and serve no kosher meat.

The Economic Environment

A well-planned marketing strategy may fail if economic times begin to change. Generic brands that reached their peak during the beginning of the decade have begun to wane as the nation has experienced better economic times.

From a pricing perspective, the consumer's elasticity of demand is important to know because pricing strategy is often contingent on such knowledge. For example, demand for gasoline and cigarettes is relatively inelastic due respectively to product need and brand loyalty. Hence, the price of each product can be raised significantly before there is a relatively larger decrease in the percentage of demand. This explains why the recent Great American gas-out was simply just out of gas.

The Political and Legal Environment

The laws of this country have a dramatic and

changing impact on marketing strategy. Consider, for example, the Lanham act, which deals with issues related to trademarks. Recently, a large Korean company was sued by Vanna White of the *Wheel of Fortune* TV game show because in a print advertisement they used a robot with a blond wig who turned letters in a game show. Vanna claimed that it was her image that was brought to mind by the robot and she was awarded damages.

Recently, the concept of "dilution" was introduced into business law. Dilution relates to the weakening or broadening of a brand's image in the mind of the average consumer. The concept behind dilution can be explained best, however, through the use of an example. Suppose that a company unaffiliated with Kodak introduces "Kodak" clothing. Kodak could take legal action against this company simply because the clothing has potentially weakened Kodak's position as a premier film manufacturer. That is, consumers may now perceive the company as both a clothing and film manufacturer, no longer as just a film specialist. It is critical that a company keep an eye on the changing legal environment as it affects its many business relationships.

THE COMPETITIVE ENVIRONMENT

A company has little control of the action taken by the competition. However, once action is taken, it is the responsibility of the company to react in some fashion. Often, market leaders feel little need to react to moves by smaller competitors. After all, they are market leaders, what could happen? Lots could happen and quickly! The competitor could dramatically drop price and gain market share, which is hard to recoup.

Similarly, the competition could add value to the product by giving a greater quantity for the same price. It is the advice of Ries and Trout (1993) that market leaders should play defense and always block strong moves by the competition. I agree, and often advise firms to anticipate responses to moves by the competition that have not yet been made. As Levitt suggests, the company itself should be developing products that make its own product obsolete. That is, it is better for your own company to introduce the next generation of a product than to let the competition do it.

THE DEMOGRAPHIC ENVIRONMENT

What are the demographic trends that will affect your company? Let's take an example and ask how a study of demographic trends in aging can assist Merck, a large pharmaceutical company, in planning for the future. One look at the aging baby boomers provides the key. What products will be needed? It doesn't take a rocket scientist to realize the great need for drugs to fight arthritis, drugs for sleep disorders, drugs that naturally fight weight gain and drugs to help alleviate added stress due to pagers, e-mail, cell phones, and other electronic leashes. Am I clairvoyant? No, I'm simply a marketer using demographic trends to predict future industry growth and product usage. You can do it, too, for your own company, and it is not limited to changes in the age distribution of your region or country. Consider other factors such as geographic shifts, educational changes and changes in racial diversity.

Managing demand states

Wouldn't it be wonderful if the demand for your product was always at the level you wanted it to be? Unfortunately, this is more of a dream than a reality. Quite simply, when demand is out of balance with supply (which is almost always the case), an effective marketer needs to bring back a state of balance. We will examine five different demand states in which imbalance between demand and supply is evident. In each case, we will propose a plan to bring consistency between these factors.

WHY NO DEMAND AND NEGATIVE DEMAND ARE CHALLENGES TO ANY MARKETER

In the case of "no demand," all or important segments of a potential target market are indifferent or uninterested in a particular product. An example would be rocks found on the desert floor or pieces of the Statue of Liberty when she was renovated for her 100th birthday in 1986. However, when the rocks are smoothed and shined and made into bookends, and pieces of the statue are emphasized as part of Americana, a demand for each product comes into existence. The goal of the marketer in this instance is to stimulate the market through the creation of a need. In the first instance, this involved a slight physical change in the form of the product, in the latter it involved a linkage of the product to an individual's emotional ties to the past. Both instances are suggestive of the need for the marketer to think "out of the box" when marketing a product.

Regarding negative demand, all or most of the potential market segments dislike the product or service and actually may pay a price to avoid it. Examples include military service and the need and motivation to vaccinate children. The marketer's goal is to convert demand from negative to positive. The Marines attempt to do this with a rather flashy ad campaign emphasizing the glory, excitement and challenge of being a leatherneck. However, conversional marketing is probably the most difficult potential demand state facing any marketer, and it is a difficult task to rely on advertising alone to change attitudes toward a product from negative to positive. This conversional process usually occurs over longer periods of time. Thankfully, the marketer is typically not faced with such a situation.

How to deal with faltering demand and irregular demand

Faltering demand (where demand for a product or service is less than its former level) is quite a common occurrence. In the absence of correctional and remedial action, there is a high likelihood of a further decline in market share. One solution would be to "re-market" the product by finding new uses for it and extending its life cycle. Some years ago, Arm & Hammer Baking Soda positioned itself as a refrigerator and drain deodorant with the result of increased sales. Creative marketers must always think about new uses and new ideas for their product or service to avoid declines in demand.

When airlines and hotels are faced with a significant increase in demand over major holidays and in the summer, they are faced with irregular demand. That is, the timing pattern of demand is marked by seasonal or volatile fluctuations. The goal here is to synchronize demand and level it out. But how can this be done? The answer lies in a manipulation of one or all of the 4 P's. For example, during the off season, prices could be slashed, or advertising could be increased. In fact, a famous clothing manufacturer recently offered triple bonus points (redeemable for merchandise) for each dollar spent during April through June, in a resoundingly effective attempt to increase demand.

THE CONCEPT OF LATENT DEMAND AND THE NEED TO BE IN CONSTANT CONTACT WITH YOUR TARGET MARKET

In many cases, a substantial number of people share a need for a product or service that does not yet exist. This is called latent demand and is often revealed during marketing research through the use of focus groups designed to uncover unmet needs.

For example, a focus group in Japan regarding VCRs came up with the suggestion of a product that automatically deletes commercials during taping. This product was quickly developed and was a commercial success. The solution to uncovering latent demand is formation of a developmental marketing process. This involves a commitment to research and development, marketing research and new product development.

Successful marketing cannot be accomplished

without being in close contact with the consumer's needs and wants. This can be accomplished through marketing research. As noted earlier, demand is typically never equal to supply and, hence, the marketer is always in motion trying to balance these forces. The company that takes a laissez-faire attitude to demand and supply forces is bound for failure.

You can automate the production of cars but you cannot automate the production of customers.

Walter Reuther

KEY 6

Why a lack of marketing research means "flying blind"

About 10 years ago, the Hilton Hotels Corporation was challenged with the goal of increasing their hotel occupancy rates for weekends. They were positioned fairly well in the consumer's mind as a business hotel and possibly, as a consequence, their occupancy rates slacked off considerably from Friday until Sunday. The issue essentially was how can the goal of increasing weekend business be accomplished and how can marketing research help the company in achieving this goal.

A nationwide marketing research study was commissioned, which found that people were more tired at the end of the weekend than at the beginning. Household chores, kids and responsibilities left for the weekend because of an ever hectic week simply drained people of both time and energy. As a result of this study, the company instituted the "Hilton Bounce-back Weekend." For the weekend, rates were dropped considerably, kids were included in the room for free and breakfast was served at no extra charge. The idea was that busy executives should bring their families to a short weekend "bounce-back"get-away at a local Hilton to relax and face the week ahead. Advertising dramatized this by showing the hectic life the average American family leads and promoting Hilton as a solution to that hectic life with families swimming, eating and enjoying life together. Hence, marketing research helped Hilton position themselves more broadly in the consumer's mind as a hotel for both business and weekend activities.

WHAT IS MARKETING RESEARCH AND WHY IS IT NEEDED?

Marketing research is the systematic gathering, recording and analyzing of data about problems relating to the marketing of goods and services. It essentially is the corporation's eyes and ears to the outside world. Marketing research helps companies react and respond to their marketing issues.

For example, for a long time, a beer company (Brand R) was having a difficult time increasing market share in New York City. They naturally wondered whether the beer had an image problem or whether the product was perceived to be inferior. To gain a perspective on the problem, a marketing research company decided to do two different taste tests with two other competitors. In the first test, Brand R and the two other brands were identified by name and consumers after tasting each of them sequentially, were asked to choose the best-tasting beer. Brand R was chosen as best tasting only 10 percent of the time (much less than the other two brands). In the second taste test using other consumers, Brand R and the other two brands were unidentified In this test, Brand R was chosen as best-tasting by 45 percent of the sample. The conclusion is that Brand R is perceived as a good-tasting beer by consumers, however, it has an image problem. Further research was then conducted to examine Brand R's image in New York City.

WHAT MAJOR RESEARCH ACTIVITIES ARE UNDERTAKEN BY COMPANIES?

In general, marketing research activities fall into three distinct categories. The first is exploratory. Here research is used to increase familiarity with a marketing problem, to establish priorities for future research and to clarify concepts. The beer

To things of a sale a sellers praise belongs.

Shakespeare, Love's Labour's Lost

taste tests described above fall into this category. Marketing research may also have a descriptive goal, which is designed to "portray the characteristics of marketing phenomena and determine their frequency of occurrence," (Kinnear and Taylor 1991). The study discussed above that was designed to examine the image of Brand A is typical of descriptive research.

Finally, marketing research studies can be

described as "causal" in nature. The goal of such research is predictive using certain (independent) variables to predict the value of a dependent measure. For example, one could use many different variables to predict beer consumption inclusive of household income, age, and gender. Typically in marketing, causal research is used to examine the predictive relationship between sales as a function of advertising expenditures.

Marketing research activities span the 4 P's of marketing. For example, Kaiser Permanente recently conducted research studies to determine the most appropriate image to convey in advertising regarding their doctors. Research also helped it determine their new tag line, "In the Hands of Doctors." That is, it was shown that many patients had significant concerns that their insurance companies and not doctors determined their quality of care. Kaiser Permanente addressed this by creating an appropriate tag line designed to allay their fears. Pricing research as well as research on product and distributional issues has helped marketers effectively serve their target market effectively and efficiently.

KEY 7

A guide for the marketing manager's involvement in the research process

Recently, an undergraduate student of mine suggested that the Mars Company should market green M&M's under the brand name "the Green Ones." I wondered out loud why Mars would even think of doing such a thing, considering that M&M's of multiple colors are infinitely more interesting than a package containing just one color! The student replied that I was missing the point and that green M&M's had an interesting reputation. My next class that day was with my Executive MBA class, a class of significantly older students than my undergraduate class. I decided to ask them about the reputation of green M&M's, and interestingly no one could tell me anything of significance. Finally, I gathered my courage and asked my undergraduate class the same question.

Everyone smiled and they told me that green M&M's are believed to have aphrodisiac qualities. One student suggested that they were a cheaper alternative to Viagra!

I was shocked, not because of the reputation of green M&M's, but rather by the dramatically different level of knowledge across the two classes. Why did the EMBA class have no knowledge of the reputation of green M&M's, but in the undergraduate class, everyone knew?

The answer lies in a key difference between the two classes, that of age. It seems that the reputation of green M&M's was developed on college and high school campuses in the early 1980's and those older than 40 simply were not in school at the time the reputation developed.

This brings about an interesting sampling issue. A researcher who would have sampled people younger than 40 would generally have found strong support for the existence of such a reputation, whereas a researcher who sampled those older than 40 would generally have found no support. What is the right answer and what does such a divergence of answers mean for the marketing manager? Quite simply, it means that the marketing manager who is typically the recipient of such marketing research studies should be aware of all the issues involved in the research process from sampling issues to assumptions about representativeness. In other words, the marketing manager should be familiar enough with marketing research concepts to question the validity and reliability of a study and to understand why extremely different answers can be found with identical questions.

So at minimum, what exactly should the marketing manager know about the marketing research process to question the validity of the findings? The paragraphs that follow address these issues:

UNDERSTANDING WHEN MARKETING RESEARCH IS NEEDED
Develop an understanding of the types of infor-

When business is good it pays to advertise; when business is bad you've got to advertise.

Anonymous

mation that can be obtained through marketing research. That is, questions regarding purchase behavior as related to the distant future or past are generally not useful. Marketing research is most applicable to those situations in which additional information about the present and recent past can help reduce a manager's uncertainty about the future.

DECIDING HOW MUCH TO SPEND ON RESEARCH

Unfortunately, many marketing managers do not see the immediate or short-term value of marketing research and in tough times tend to cut marketing research expenditures first. Interestingly, the cost of doing an entire project can often be closely approximated by the research proposal. When the proposal is presented, the marketing manager should be able to determine if the information to be provided is worth the proposed expenditure.

INSURING THAT THE DATA COLLECTED IS RELEVANT TO THE DECISION BEING MADE

Andreason (1985) has suggested a process called "backward marketing research" in which synthetic data from the proposed study is generated prior to its collection to give the client an idea of what the actual data from the study might look like. Often, when the marketing manager sees such data, it becomes obvious that other questions should have been asked to address the research question or other analyses should have been completed. It is important to note that backward marketing research does not involve the falsification of data, but rather the generation of synthetic data for the sole purpose of helping the marketing manager visualize what actual data might look like from the proposed study.

SELECTING THE MOST APPROPRIATE FORMAT FOR PRESENTING THE RESEARCH

More complicated is not always better. Sometimes the best way to present data is in its simplest form. This means that pie charts and histograms often can work wonders in helping a novice in marketing research to understand complex findings.

The importance of
understanding the consumer:
Part 1

Exactly 150 years after the gold rush of 1849, the gold rush of 1999 may be about to begin. How do I know this? Why my knowledge of marketing and consumer behavior of course! Consumers are fearful that as Y2k approaches there will be massive bank failures, problems in the distribution of even basic food items and potentially a collapse in international trade, particularly with countries who are unprepared for the crisis. So what are consumers going to do? Some may only be concerned, others may worry and still others may panic. With the potential of a failure in the banking system, barter may become a reality. What better to barter with than precious metals? Gold may be in for a dramatic short-term rise in price, despite its increasing abundance in supply.

What factors influence consumer purchase decisions? There are essentially two main categories of factors composed of intra and inter-personal variables. Intra-individual variables will be covered in this key and inter-personal variables in Key 9.

These factors are composed of motivation, perception, learning, and attitudes. We will briefly review each one. According to Maslow, everyone is motivated by needs and wants. Maslow defined a hierarchy of needs, which range from physiological to safety to a feeling of belonging and love to self esteem and finally self actualization. One product can satisfy many needs at once, such as a hamburger eaten in a social environment. Generally, it is in the interest of the marketer to associate the product with a higher level need. That is, beer certainly can be positioned as satisfying a need for thirst, but often a beer tries to establish an image linked to a more sophisticated need. Lowenbrau has an imported German image, which through conspicuous consumption may send a message to others that the person who drinks it is sophisticated. Indeed, Sirgy (1982) has shown that consumers project their image through the brands they purchase.

Perception is the process by which a person selects, organizes and interprets informational inputs to create a meaningful picture of the world.

For example, we use the process of selective perception to screen out ideas, messages and information not relevant to us. This means that in the ever cluttered world of advertising, it is imperative that the advertiser break through the clutter to get the message through to the consumer. Often this can be accomplished through the use of celebrity spokespeople.

Learning is what is remembered. We buy products we have had a favorable experience with and avoid products that we evaluate unfavorably. It is in the marketer's best interest to create and encourage brand loyalty through the learning process. If trial can be induced, a favorable experience will typically result in a repurchase of the same brand as the consumer turns on the loyalty switch to avoid thinking about the purchase decision.

Attitudes are directed toward objects, people, places or events and represent feelings and predispositions in which people believe strongly enough in that they are willing to take action. They are typically viewed as a precursor to behavior (with some exceptions), where a favorable attitude leads to purchase and an unfavorable one does not. Hence, they are extremely important in marketing and advertising strategy.

In marketing and advertising, we are typically focused on attitude change toward products and brands. Attitude toward a product or brand can be changed typically through an adaptation of a product (e.g., tuna is now dolphin safe) or a repositioning of the brand in its advertising.

For example, Michelin tires emphasized its safety through its tag line and imagery: "There's a lot riding on your tires," and the picture of a baby playing inside of the tire.

Arm & Hammer created a more favorable attitude toward its baking soda by finding and emphasizing a new product usage, that of refreshing the odor of a kitchen drain. It is important to note, however, that a favorable attitude is not always linked to purchase. That is, I have a favorable attitude toward a Mercedes-Benz, but no money to purchase it.

The importance of understanding the consumer: Part 2

As one drives down the streets of Los Angeles, it is quickly evident that the sports utility vehicle is extremely popular. Everyone who aspires to be someone has one. Interestingly, the trend has been to buy a bigger and bigger vehicle. The mode at first was the Jeep Cherokee. This was replaced by the Ford Explorer, then the Range Rover, followed by the Ford Expedition, the GMC Suburban and finally the Hummer. Believe it or not, on the near horizon is the Ford Excursion, which will measure 6.5 feet wide and get just a handful of miles per gallon. So the question must be asked, how come people are willing to dish out $50,000 or more for a car that gets approximately eight miles to the gallon on average, harms the environment and is designed for the rough terrain typically encountered in the outback, not the shopping mall? The answer lies in the inter-personal variable influences on consumer behavior.

INTER-PERSONAL INFLUENCERS OF CONSUMER PURCHASE DECISIONS

These factors include reference groups, family

People will buy any product that has been made smaller if it retains the functionality of the larger product and has a handle.

Eri Golenlo, P.C. Magazine

and culture. Reference groups are composed of people whom the individual looks to when forming attitudes and beliefs. One emulates certain reference groups (aspirational groups) whereas one is actually a member of other groups (membership groups). For example, the impact of the use of celebrities in advertising is largely due to their aspirational effect on consumers. Young kids buy Adidas to be like Kobe Bryant. Yuppies with cell phones, dark glasses and a mug of Starbuck's coffee are influenced to buy Range Rovers to be like their neighbors, family members or close friends (all membership groups).

Bourne (1957) actually classified products and brands more than 40 years ago as to the degree of influence of reference groups on purchase behavior. His general conclusion was that brands and product categories that are more closely linked to socialization processes are more strongly influenced by reference groups. Hence, cigarettes qualify on a brand and product basis, whereas toilet paper does not. Friends do not take exception to you if you buy Charmin as opposed to Scott.

Reference groups have two important functions. First, they influence a person's attitudes and self concept and, second, they create pressures for conformity. If a product is identified as strongly influenced by reference groups, the marketer might use this in advertising designed to show social acceptance if you buy or consume a particular brand. Note that almost all beer advertising takes this approach (i.e., "Miller time").

The family also has a big influence on consumer behavior. The husband's or wife's dominance regarding a purchase decision has been shown to vary as a function of product category. In addition, for a given product category the husband has been shown to dominate on some issues and the wife on others. For example, although the husband may decide that it is time to buy a new car, the wife may influence the purchase of various attributes in the car. Children also influence purchases of the family, particularly in areas relevant to them (i.e., family dining-out choices, cereals and toys). The implications for marketers regarding family influence is that one should be aware of which member of the family dominates a purchase decision, typically down to the attribute level. If such information is known, then marketing communications can be targeted to the appropriate person in the family who is influencing that part of the decision.

Finally, culture is extremely important in purchase decisions. Culture is defined as the whole set of beliefs, attitudes and ways of doing things of a reasonably homogeneous set of people. However, the study of culture is not that simple, as many sub-cultures exist in a given society. For example, sales of bread in the Brighton Beach area of Brooklyn and in the Fairfax area of Los Angeles dropped to next to nothing recently.

Had everyone gone on a special diet? Well, sort of. These areas are well known to be inhabited by a large Jewish population who celebrate Passover. Since matzoth must be consumed instead of bread during this time period, the reason is obvious why bread sales declined. The marketer must be aware of local customs, not only when conducting international marketing, but also in terms of domestic marketing. The consumer is a complex person who may not always seem to be acting in a rational way.

An understanding of the intra- and inter-personal variables that effect consumer behavior help to explain how supposed irrationality can be interpreted.

Why selling to the entire market may not be a good idea

Often it seems reasonable to sell your product to the entire market. After all, why leave anyone out? However, just like a politician, it is difficult to be all things to everyone. Typically, if you attempt to be everything to everyone, your image becomes cloudy. Let's take a case in point. Around 15 years ago, the Gap was a clothing store that sold colorful t-shirts and blue jeans. If you asked me to describe the differential advantage of the Gap versus the competition, I would have been hard pressed to find one. Today things are very different. We have a Gap store for all ages. There is Baby Gap, Gap for Kids and, of course, Gap.

Not only that, there is a Gap-owned store for each income level and life style ranging from Old Navy for relatively inexpensive clothing to Banana Republic on the high end. It is relatively easy now for the consumer to notice the distinctive image and characteristic of each Gap store, simply because Gap has effectively segmented the market. But consumers are not the only ones who have noticed the success of Gap. Wall Street has also as the stock has shown tremendous gains. So the question remains, what is market segmentation all about and how could it be used in your business?

UNDERSTANDING MARKET SEGMENTATION

Market segmentation is the subdivision of a market into distinct subsets of consumers, where any subset may be selected as a target market to be reached with a distinctive marketing mix. Quite simply, it is the process of identifying groups of buyers with different purchasing needs or requirements. For example, those who buy from Banana Republic may be looking for clothes with style and pizzazz, whereas those who purchase from Old Navy may be looking for value. By segmenting a market, one can gain a larger presence in a smaller part of the total market.

THE MARKET SEGMENTATION PROCESS

The process of segmentation involves five steps. First, one must identify (typically) through market research the salient characteristics that can identify distinct market segments. Some of the more obvious are gender, age and income. Virginia Lights are the cigarette for women, and Tab is the cola for women. Diet Coke was originally positioned as the cola for men. Sound ridiculous? Maybe not. Remember that over time, perception becomes reality. The second step is to determine the size and value of the various potential segments on factors, such as purchase rate, family size, extent of competition, etc.

Next is a closer focus on the competition, and a determination of how they are positioned in the market. Home Base's current challenges do not necessarily relate to internal issues, their current challenge is Home Depot, a larger and stronger competitor from whom they are not distinctly differentiated.

A fourth step involves looking for opportunities consisting of market segments not being served by existing brands. The tuna fish brand that was the first to claim that it was dolphin safe made great headway with consumers who were environmentally conscious. Finally, once a segment is identified, correlated characteristics of the segment must be identified. For example, if you have just entered the market with an all-natural toothpaste, demographic, geographic and/or psychographic characteristics of potential consumers should be identified.

THE ADVANTAGES OF SEGMENTATION

As noted earlier, market segmentation allows one to be a larger fish in a smaller market. This creates many advantages in and of itself. First, because you are targeted to a specific market, the marketer is in a better position to spot, compare and adjust to always changing marketing opportunities. It is easier to examine the needs of the segment in light of the offering of competitors. In addition, the seller can more easily develop marketing programs and budgets based upon a clearer idea of the response characteristics of specific market segments as opposed to the entire market.

DIFFERENT WAYS TO SEGMENT MARKETS

The brand, Cycle, used a creative segmentation process to capture market share in dog food. While their competitors sold the same dog food to any dog who came along, Cycle realized that even dogs could be segmented on distinguishable characteristics, such as weight, and age. The result: The competition's share went to the dogs.

Other factors such as life style, personality factors, benefits sought, user rate and user status are also effective segmentation factors. When Schaefer says that they are "The one beer to have when you're having more than one," it is clear that their market segment, nicely put, is the heavy beer drinker.

By far, the most frequently used segmentation factors are demographic in nature, including age, gender, family size, income, occupation, education level, family life cycle stage, religion and nationality for international marketing. The frequency that demographic factors are used can be simply explained. First, they are highly associated with consumer wants or usage rates and, second, these variables are easy to measure.

How to generate repeat purchases

One of the key differences between selling and marketing is that marketers are concerned about repurchase behavior and the development of brand loyalty, whereas in selling, the key goal is simply to move the product.

A key question is how to encourage repurchase behavior? One obvious answer is that if product quality is good, the product will sell itself. However, the path to success is littered with many companies who have developed a better mousetrap only to see other companies succeed where they failed. So from a strategic perspective, how can one encourage brand loyalty and repurchase?

DEALING WITH POST-PURCHASE DISSATISFACTION

How many times have you purchased an expensive product and instead of feeling good about yourself, spent the time debating whether you made the right choice? This behavior is called "cognitive dissonance" and is linked to cognition (or thought) that is dissonant (or clashing). Dissonance is particularly present for decisions that are involved or important and for which the unchosen alternatives are particularly attractive. But how is it resolved? Often, the consumer searches for information that supports the decision, however, along the way, information may be uncovered that is contrary to the chosen alternative.

A creative marketer knows that when a purchase is particularly involved or costly, dissonance is typically present and the consumer will likely engage in a post-purchase information search about chosen and unchosen alternatives. However, instead of allowing the consumer to seek out information, information that supports the chosen alternative should be provided by the manufacturer.

For example, when I bought my Saturn I had concerns that I should have purchased a Honda Civic. These concerns were allayed to some degree by the dealer, who sent me favorable information (post-purchase) about the car and who congratulated me on what he called a "smart purchase," which he stated "will pay-off for the life of the car." Every six months I am called by someone at the dealership regarding how the car is holding up. This concern by the dealer reinforces my feeling that someone cares at Saturn and that I made the correct choice.

THE EFFECTIVE USE OF INCENTIVES

Another way to encourage repeat purchase is through marketing incentives. For example, many companies have programs that reward customers for frequent purchases. United's Mileage Plus comes to mind. In an industry where it is difficult to differentiate the product (i.e., many airlines can get you from New York City to Los Angeles), frequent-flyer programs encourage the consumer to continue flying with one company to reap rewards. Splitting loyalty between airlines may not be prudent because it may take twice as long to accumulate mileage to receive free flights.

Other companies reward consumers with points that accumulate after every purchase. These points can be cashed in for free merchandise once certain levels are reached. The Broadway, a former Los Angeles department store, often used this tactic to encourage repeat purchase. Many of my students have claimed that L.L. Bean, the famous mail-order rugged clothing manufacturer, should consider the same approach. A natural name for the program would be "Bean Counters."

The first law in advertising

is to avoid the concrete

promote and promote the

delightfully vague.

John Crosby, **New York Times**

Establishing a brand name is a key strategic advantage

W hen I was a child, my grandmother would always insist on buying Bayer aspirin. I remember telling her that all aspirins are alike.

She would reply, "They all may be alike, but Bayer is different." When I pressed her to explain the difference, she could not respond except to say that Bayer is better. In my mind this example illustrated the power of a brand name. Brands distinguish a product from the competition and enable the marketer to build an image.

WHAT ADVANTAGES DO BRANDS OFFER?

Aside from those advantages discussed in the paragraph above, branding has other benefits. A brand can become associated with specific attributes. For example, Volvo is known for safety, while Mercedes is known for craftsmanship. The brand name can also be used to launch new products. Marlboro used their cowboy image to come out with a line of rugged clothing, while

Tropicana attempted to extend their strength in orange juice into other juices. The brand name also insulates the company from price sensitivity on behalf of the consumer. That is, because of the brand's reputation, consumers may be more hesitant to switch to another brand given a price increase, especially if brand loyalty has developed. Brand identification also insures shelf placement and other advantages in the distribution process. Proctor and Gamble has significant distribution power because of the strength of their brand name and because of this, the company's products often get good placement in stores.

WHAT ARE THE COMPONENTS THAT MAKE AN EFFECTIVE BRAND NAME?

An effective brand name should achieve many different objectives. First and foremost, it should suggest something about the product's benefits. The brand name is often described as supplying the consumer with a "chunk" of information about the product. It is always helpful if that information contains a description of the product. For example, it is clear what Shake and Bake does. Likewise, Coldspot is an effective brand name for a refrigerator. Some companies have also attempted to name their product with the first letter of the key benefit it supplies. For example, Sealy, Serta, Spring Air, and Stearns & Foster all begin with S, which coincidentally is the same first letter in SLEEP! Finally, a brand name should be easy to pronounce and remember. Hence, shorter names are better. Consider the detergent area with names such as Tide, Duz, Cheer, Era, and Wisk. Arguably, even Sylvester Stallone understood this branding principle, producing short one-name movies whose titles could be easily remembered. Rocky and Rambo come to mind. Don't ever be in the position where you have chosen a brand name that is easily forgotten, such as the artist formally known as Prince!

FOCUSING ON COMPANY NAME VERSUS BRAND NAME

In many instances, the strategy of the firm is to emphasize the company name as a brand instead of creating a specific brand name. General Electric pursues this strategy as does Saturn and Heinz. Typically, the logic behind this approach is that the company name is strong and is distinguishable in and of itself. Saturn uses the company name strategy because it wishes to promote a family image and unity within and between the company and the consumer. It is Saturn's belief that brand names would detract from their goal of creating a large "Saturn" family. Saturn's current slogan of "Different kind of company, a different kind of car" reflects this positioning. (As an aside, this author once suggested to Saturn that they change their slogan to . . . "At Saturn, we run rings around the competition." They looked at me like I came from outer space).

Those companies who pursue individual brand names may believe that the brand should develop an image on its own. That is, if something negative happens to the company, there is less of a likelihood of the negativity being spread down to the brand level.

In fact, Procter & Gamble's strategy of focusing on brand names helped them when rumors spread regarding a supposed association of the company with a devil worshiping sect.

The inherent advantage of the pioneer brand

Many companies promote that they were the first in the product class or that they invented the product class. For example, Chrysler in the day of Lee Iacocca used to promote that it invented the minivan. Ries and Trout (1993) in their book titled *The 22 Immutable Laws of Marketing*, argue for the advantage of pioneer brands. In a humorous approach to the power of the pioneer they ask, "What's the name of the first person to fly the Atlantic Ocean solo?" The answer, *of course*, is Charles Lindbergh. However, they make a point that identifying the second person to fly the Atlantic ocean solo is not so easy. The answer, of course, is Bert Hinkler. These authors propose two laws that support the pioneer advantage. First is the Law of Leadership: It's better to be first than to be better. Second is the law of the category: If you can't be first in a category, set up a new category you can be first in. But why is pioneering so important?

WHY IS IT IMPORTANT TO BE A PIONEER BRAND?
Ries and Trout's humorous example gives a clue

as to why pioneering is important. Quite simply, the pioneer brand is remembered best among alternative brands. Academic research also supports this point (Kardes and Kalyanaram 1992). The reason is clear, because the pioneer is first in its category, its features are perceived as more novel and attention-drawing for the consumer. The pioneer offers other advantages that follower brands cannot duplicate. That is, the pioneer sets the consumers expectations about the product class. Essentially, it becomes the category prototype to which all other brands are compared (usually unfavorably). Pioneer brands, because they are first in the market, can take the best position in the market.

This first position allows the pioneer brand to create barriers to entry for other brands. Finally, if people experience the pioneer brand first and like it, they may stay with the brand resulting in continued brand loyalty.

It is important to note that in a given product class, only one brand can claim to be the pioneer. All other brands are by definition followers. This is why Ries and Trout suggest that if one cannot be the pioneer brand in a category, then invent a category in which one can become the pioneer.

As an example, Häagen-Dazs was not the first ice cream in America, but it can claim to be the first gourmet ice cream from the exotic land called New Jersey!

How can the pioneer brand advantage be maintained over time?

Considering that the pioneer brand advantage is unique to a given brand and is not replicable within a product class, it is important to emphasize it in various marketing communications about the brand. Quite simply, my advice can be summarized as follows: Let consumers know it; don't let them forget it. This can be done through an emphasis in advertising (a la' Chrysler) or on packaging. The way the pioneer status is emphasized can be done using terms such as "the First," "World's First," "The original," or indeed "the Pioneer". Research is still inconclusive as to which label is best (Alpert and Kamins 1995).

Doing business without advertising is like winking at a girl in the dark. You may know what you are doing but nobody else does.

Stuart Henderson Britt,
New York Herald Tribune

How can the follower
brand compete?

The discussion of the prior chapter would make it seem that any brand that is not the pioneer in its product class could not effectively compete. Let's face it, in most cases your brand will follow the pioneer into a product class.

So what follows is a discussion of how to compete against a pioneer brand and gain an advantage. Competing against the pioneer has been successful in the past. Golder and Tellis (1993) have documented that the pioneer advantage is not insurmountable. Indeed, there are many instances across different product categories in which the pioneer is no longer the market leader, or worse, is no longer in the market at all. I outline strategies for follower brands below.

POSITION NEAR OTHER FOLLOWERS AND NOT DIRECTLY AGAINST THE PIONEER

Carpenter and Nakamoto (1989, p. 297) argue that follower brands should try to be distinct and position away from the pioneer. They claim that when a follower brand is positioned too close to the pioneer they are overshadowed. A better strategy, according to the authors, would be to segment the market, "copying a differentiated entrant rather than the pioneer. . . . It enables both late entrants to develop a degree of prominence, reduce their own price sensitivity, and increase the price sensitivity of the pioneer."

EMPHASIZE NEWNESS
One of the greatest perceptual weaknesses that consumers have of the pioneer brand is that because it came out before other brands, it may not be up-to-date on the newest technological developments in the product class (Alpert and Kamins, 1994). This means that the follower brand should emphasize its quality by positioning itself as newer or newest on the market and, hence, more attune to consumer preferences. A reasonable positioning for the follower brand would be new and improved over the competition.

ENTER THE MARKET QUICKLY AFTER THE PIONEER
The shorter the period of time that the pioneer brand is alone in the market the less its pioneer advantage. It is imperative that follower brands enter the market as soon as possible after the pioneer. This can negate the pioneer advantage. Be a fast follower!

MARKET LEADERSHIP IS ALSO AN ADVANTAGE AND ATTAINABLE BY THE FOLLOWER BRAND
My research has shown that consumer perceptions of the market leader are even more favorable than that of the pioneer brand. The market leader is distinguishable and unique. Compaq computer makes it clear in its advertisements and packaging that they are the worldwide market leader in sales of PC's. The inference by the consumer is that if

you sell more than the competition, then you must be better. The tough part of this market leadership strategy is how does one become the leader in the first place? We'll discuss this later.

Can new products give new life to companies?

I n August, 1998, I purchased a new Compaq Presario computer with a monitor and printer. By the time I got it shipped and out of the box, it was outdated. My friends were already telling me how poorly my computer stacked up against the one they were going to buy one month later. I felt terrible, angry and depressed and felt that I should have waited. But if I waited, it would be the same scenario, only delayed. The problem here is that the product life cycle is shrinking at a rate faster than in any time in our history.

This means that products move from product development, to introduction, to growth, to maturity and then decline at lightening speed. What does this all mean?

UNDERSTANDING THE PRODUCT LIFE CYCLE

The life cycle starts with product development. It is here where new ideas are generated and it is here where 95 percent or more of these ideas are killed before they see the light of day. If a product makes it into the introduction stage, sales growth is typically slow because the market needs to understand the product and it takes time for people to realize that a new product is present. Compounding the difficulty for the marketer at the introduction stage is that often development costs are extensive and so profits are extremely negative at this stage. For example, Agouron Pharmaceuticals, maker of Viracept (an effective treatment for the H.I.V. virus), had many Stage III drug failures before launching this one successful drug. This is why many start-up biotechnology firms go belly-up. It's not for lack of ideas, but rather for lack of funds.

Growth is a period of increasingly rapid market expansion and acceptance. It is at the latter part of this stage when profits begin to turn positive as sales may increase at breakneck speed. When the product reaches the maturity stage, many competitors have typically entered the market, sales level off and profits begin to peak and decline as investment must be made in marketing activities to maintain a competitive position. Decline is the period where both sales and profits decline for various reasons inclusive of market saturation as well as attack from new and better products.

THE SHRINKAGE OF THE PRODUCT LIFE CYCLE
It only stands to reason that as the time from product development to decline shortens, the pressure to produce new products increases. Why?

The reason is that there is only a narrow period in the product life cycle when the company is making profits (typically from late growth to maturity). Therefore, as that period shrinks, there is pressure to produce new products, which begin their journey through the life cycle, hitting the "sweet spot" in which profits are made. It is not easy to continually introduce new and improved products and convince the consumer that such products are needed or wanted. Hence, because the product life cycle is shrinking, the marketing and business environment is more competitive than it ever was! In fact, executives at Intel have made the point that each time they introduce a new chip they are betting the life of the company on the decision.

Why New Products Often Fail and How to Minimize the Risk

Flavored catsup, Cue toothpaste (introduced in France), 100-pound bags of dog food, and blood-red orange juice. What do these products have in common? They all failed. Why do new products fail? Many times top executives have a brilliant idea, which comes from the top of their heads. Because it is the chief executive, no one ever has the courage to question it and the product becomes a reality. However, when consumers found the 100-pound sacks of dog food to be too heavy to lift, the company found the chief executive light enough to carry him out the door.

When Cue toothpaste did not sell in France, a little research found out that the pronunciation and spelling of the name was the same as the part of the body one sits on. Not enough research on foreign customs and behaviors can be deadly when doing international marketing and has been the cause of many product failures. Such a problem can also exist in the United States, where strawberry-flavored catsup and blood-red orange juice was found to be distasteful to Americans. A lack of marketing research and knowledge of the right questions to ask was the cause of this problem. Products also fail due to other reasons: The market may be overestimated, competitors present a difficult challenge, price was too low or too high or the positioning was incorrect. The positioning of Alaska Airlines as a quality airline backfired when consumers perceived it to be a high-priced airline. Today most of Alaska's advertising focuses on low price as opposed to quality to correct this misperception.

How can one cut down the failure rate of new products? The answer lies in effective marketing research and a continual ear to the desires and product benefits sought by consumers. Avoid new product decisions as a function of a sample size of one. The chief executive does not always have the right idea; it is your target market that ultimately has the power. Also, creative approaches to new product development also increase the success rate. Goldenberg, Mazursky and Solomon (1999) suggest that applying what they call "creativity templates" to the new product development process results in the creation of dramatically new products. For example, using the template of replacement, what new form of chair could be developed by *replacing* its legs. It becomes obvious that the swing, beach chair and baby seat attached to a table all are chairs without traditional legs. Here's an exercise: can you think of a new form of chair without legs?

KEY 16

Issues relating to effective product strategy

The Honda Motor Company produced relatively inexpensive cars around 25 years ago, so did Toyota. The roads of California were cluttered with little Civic CVCC's and Corolla's. Today, the image of Honda and Toyota has changed dramatically in the mind of the consumer. First, both companies offer many more models and a broader range of choice for the consumer. Second, both companies offer luxury divisions (Acura is linked to Honda and Lexus to Toyota).

Today, both Honda and Toyota benefited from creative marketing thinking of a quarter century ago. Both companies took a broader perspective of their market and asked themselves the question, "How will the needs of our current CVCC and Corolla buyer change over time?" These brands provided basic but reliable transportation in 1975, but is that what will be required by these consumers in 1980, 1990 and 2000? Clearly, the answer to this question was no. Both Toyota and

Honda grew and matured over time with their consumer base. They introduced more luxurious models slowly and introduced cars that were essentially segmented on a use basis. For example, the Prelude was a sporty car, the Accord was a larger mid-size car and the Del Sol was a small sports car. Creative marketers think creatively not only for today but also for tomorrow. Below we discuss some strategic product decisions that can be applied for the present as well as the future.

Should we consider stretching or shrinking our product line?

What Honda and Toyota did was stretch their product line to the upside over a period of 25 years by introducing more expensive models. What, however, triggers a stretch? Let's take the case where a company wishes to add cheaper models to their current line—a downward stretch. Why might this occur? First, the company might find severe competition at the market's high side and enters the lower end where market growth might be more dramatic. Second, the company might enter the lower end to fill a hole in their line, which could have been an inroad for the competition.

However, a line stretch is not always easy to accomplish. First of all, if a high-quality product begins to produce cheaper items, this may reflect on the image of the company as a whole. For example, Pierre Cardin began to apply his name to a set of five-piece luggage that cost $99. The luggage manufacturer thought that the Pierre Cardin name would enhance the quality perception of the luggage. It may have, but alternatively the risk is that the image of Pierre Cardin can easily sink to new lows. Another problem of a line stretch is that the new product may eat into the sales of the existing product. For example, when Ford introduces the new gigantic sports utility vehicle, will sales of the existing Expedition and Explorer suffer. Finally, existing dealers may be unwilling or unable to handle the new products, introducing problems that previously did not exist.

BRAND EXTENSIONS—WHAT SITUATIONS CONTRIBUTE TO THEIR SUCCESS?

The idea behind a brand extension strategy is that customers will accept the new product because they are already familiar with the brand name. Although this seems reasonable, such a strategy becomes questionable if the consumer cannot link the original product with the new one. For example, Kodak has achieved some success in making lenses for eyeglasses because of the consumer's perception of its expertise in making lenses for cameras. But is the connection that obvious between Microsoft's image as a software producer and children's interactive toys?

Again, the key to a successful brand extension is the link made between the original product and the extension in the consumer's mind. Do not be limited into thinking that product extensions should have the same function as the original product. For example, what is the link between Harley Davidson Motorcycles and Harley Davidson cigarettes? The answer lies in the rugged or tough lifestyle both convey. Linkage is a broader concept than just product function.

KEY 17

Pricing could be tricky.
What should I charge?

Prices for American silver coins have risen considerably since the beginning of 1999. On January 1, $1 in silver coins would cost around $4. Five months later, the price had risen 25 percent to $5. What will the price be as we approach the turning point of the millenium?

Many coin dealers have not adjusted their price fast enough to meet market demand. Hence, the gap between what you would normally pay for silver and what you could sell it for has narrowed. The same phenomena happened 20 years ago when the Hunt brothers cornered the silver market.

WHY PRICING IS IMPORTANT
Of the 4 P's discussed in Key 1, only price generates revenue; all of the other P's are costs. Hence, finding the right price to sell to the target market is extremely important. If you charge too much, you may price yourself out of the market; pricing too low may cause your company to deflate it's image.

PRICING AS A CUE FOR THE CONSUMER

Many people judge quality through the price of the product. Essentially, the price of a product signals quality. This price/quality relationship has been shown to be strongest when the consumer lacks product experience, the purchase is perceived to be risky and when there is little basis for making direct product comparisons. Regarding the latter, there have been many experiments in the marketing literature where consumers are asked to use an unbranded product described as inexpensive and then to rate it. They are then given another identical product priced considerably higher and asked to rate it. The catch in the experiment is that the product is the same across conditions (the consumer is unaware of this), only its price and packaging has been changed. Many such studies have been done for beer because it is difficult for consumers to establish its overall quality.

The results are that the more expensive beer is rated significantly higher on taste characteristics and purchase intention than the less expensive beer. Why does this happen if the beer is all the same? It is because price serves as a indicator of quality for a product in which quality is often nebulous.

PRICING STRATEGIES

An attempt to teach how to set price for a product or product line is beyond the scope of this book. However, pricing can either be cost-oriented or demand-oriented. Pricing on the basis of cost is very tricky simply because variable cost changes as a function of the number of units sold and the number of units sold is often a function of price. The key to demand-oriented pricing is that it focuses on the buyer's perception of value as opposed to the seller's level of cost.

Hence, in a simple form, if the average consumer perceives that a product is of significantly higher quality than the largest competitor, then a product probably can have a significantly higher price than the competition. The key is to quantify the quality advantage of the product versus the competition.

One approach would be to use a diagnostic method, where the product and the competition are evaluated on a series of attributes (typically on a 1–7 scale where 7 = excellent and 1 = poor). These attributes are then weighted by their importance, such that the importance scores across attributes sum to 1. The weighted evaluation is then summed across attributes for each brand and then compared across brands. So for example, let's say that after this process is completed, your product scores a 35 and your main competitor scores a 30. This means that you have a (35-30)/30 or 16.67 percent perceived quality advantage over your main competitor. Arguably, your product could charge up to 16.67 percent higher than the competition. Other techniques are also available to quantify the perceived quality advantage, but they are also beyond the scope of this book.

Effective ways to promote your product

Look, up in the sky, it's a bird, it's a plane, no it's . . . a 10,000 pound ape clinging to New York's World Trade Center. This was an actual promotional device used by Dino De Laurentiis years ago to gain the world's attention for the remake of King Kong. This example should make it clear that promotion is not just traditional advertising, but rather is much broader in scope. In fact, promotion is an umbrella concept that consists of advertising, personal selling, sales promotion and public relations (of which King Kong is an example).

THE ELEMENTS OF PROMOTION

Advertising: Any paid form of non-personal presentation of goods or services by an identified sponsor. It comes in many forms inclusive of internet, television print, billboard, direct mail, etc.

Personal selling: This form of promotion involves interpersonal relationships between customers and potential sellers through sales-people. Where advertising can gain your attention, personal selling is often needed to close a deal, especially for high-ticket items or industrial goods.

Sales promotion: This type of promotion involves short term incentives to encourage the purchase of a product or service. Examples include coupons, end of aisle displays, and free gifts with purchase. The free gift with purchase concept has been made popular by many perfume companies here and abroad.

Public relations: Here the goal is to build good relationships with one's various publics, by obtaining favorable publicity to enhance image or bring attention to the product or service. Public relations can be a very effective promotional tool because it is typically not viewed by consumers in a cynical light as advertising tends to be. For example, in Hollywood, product placement in movies and television shows has become a big industry. Here the firm attempts to get the studio to use real products in movies. For example, Pierce Brosnan as James Bond drove the new BMW Boxster in the movie "Goldeneye." Although this was not an overt advertisement, it significantly influenced many people who wished to convey the image of Bond by driving his car. Sales of this model rose after the movie came out.

THE GOALS OF PROMOTION

The naive person would say that the goal of promotion, just like the goal of advertising, is to sell the product. While this is the ultimate goal, there are other stages before a sale can occur. That is, one must first be made aware of the product or service (cognitive stage); then develop a liking or preference for the product (affective stage), and that finally results in action or purchase (conative stage). The most effective promotional approach differs for each stage.

To create awareness, sales promotion, public relations and advertising are effective. Enhancing preference for the product is typically best achieved through the use of comparative advertising and personal selling. Finally, the effort to motivate purchase is typically done through personal selling and some forms of advertising.

Lavidge and Steiner (1961) outlined the critical steps that need to be covered in any advertising evaluation program. Their findings are also applicable to the broader category of promotion. They stated:

1 Determine what steps are most critical in a particular case, that is, what the steps leading to purchase are for most consumers.

2 Determine how many people are, at the moment, on which steps.

3 Determine which people on which steps it is most important to reach.

With the knowledge as outlined above, the marketing manager can plan a promotional strategy tailored exactly to the target market.

Advertising as a promotional tool

Think for a moment about your favorite advertisement of all time. We all have one and we think fondly about it. Mine is the advertisement for Coca-Cola when Mean Joe Greene of the Pittsburgh Stealers gives the shirt off his back to a young kid for a sip of Coke. Advertising is powerful and can create long-lasting images in our mind.

MAJOR TYPES OF ADVERTISING

Advertisements can be classified into three major forms: informative, persuasive, and reminder. We will cover each type below.

Informative advertising: This type achieves two goals, that of alerting consumers to the existence of a new product or service and ultimately in providing information about the product or service so that a need and a preference is created.

Persuasive: This type of advertising is designed

to influence purchase. Persuasive advertising can be of four forms. First, it can be described as comparative or noncomparative. Comparative ads mention the competition, whereas noncomparative ads do not. It is advised that market leaders in a category not mention the competition in their advertising. Put simply, if you are already the leader, then why mention your competitor? Persuasive ads can also be described as being either one-sided or two-sided. One-sided ads are typical in that only favorable attributes are mentioned about the product. Two-sided ads mention product limitations on unimportant attributes, so that credibility is enhanced.

Reminder: This form of advertising is important after a purchase has been made so that the product is continually in the mind of the consumer. The "Coke is it!" advertising campaign is an example of this approach.

ADVERTISING PITFALLS

Advertising can be an effective communication device, although there are always potential problems. For example, if one advertises excessively, the advertising campaign could suffer from wearout. That is, the target market has viewed the ad so many times that it no longer makes a positive impression, and, in fact, it may make a negative impression in the form of an annoyance. This suggests that advertisers should continually measure the effectiveness of their advertising on such factors as recall, attitude and ability to influence and motivate purchase.

Many advertisers also use celebrities as product spokespeople. Although this can be an effective tactic because it helps one's advertisement to cut through the clutter, approach the use of celebrities with caution. Often, celebrities may have their own agenda and sell a multitude of products. When this happens, the consumer may attribute the celebrity's personal link to your product as a function of money as opposed to a real liking for the merchandise. Moreover, celebrities may go through difficult times or become controversial and then their endorsement becomes less valuable. O.J. Simpson, Michael Jackson, Anita Bryant and Madonna come to mind as examples.

Finally, there must be a congruence or fit between the celebrity and the product (Kamins and Gupta 1994). This fit is linked to the celebrity's image in the movies or their image in real life. For example, Leonard Nimoy (Mr. Spock of *Star Trek* fame) and computers would be a great fit. However, imagine the pitfall of using Madonna as a spokeswoman for *Modern Maturity* magazine or Yul Brynner as a spokesman for a dandruff shampoo.

A final pitfall in advertising is the use of exaggeration. Advertisers are tempted to exaggerate the characteristics and performance of their product. This temptation should be ignored as research has shown that it is better to present your product in a realistic light than to dramatically exaggerate it. Ratings of product attitude and purchase intention was shown to be higher for those who saw an advertisement that realistically presented product characteristics than for one that used exaggeration or extreme puffery (Kamins and Assael 1987).

Distribution as an effective component of marketing strategy

Once upon a time, way before the frenzy with the Furby, there was a frenzy with a doll called Cabbage Patch. Each Cabbage Patch doll was different and came with its own birth certificate. Consumers were waiting in line in droves to buy a doll, some even went to England to buy the dolls and sell them at a profit back in the United States. Others got into fist fights while in line waiting to purchase the doll. Why did all of this happen? Part of the answer is that products become faddish, hot one moment and cold the next. Other toys that became faddish are Teddy Ruxspin, Tickle-Me Elmo, hula hoops and yoyo's.

What causes a product to become faddish? Arguably, the product should be different and unique in some fashion. Another key factor may be tied to distribution strategy. That is, if a product becomes suddenly in demand, it may be in the marketer's interest to stay just a bit behind demand so that consumer's have to make a considerable effort to purchase the product. This keeps the madness going, so to speak. If consumers are finally able to purchase the product, they see it as an accomplishment and even if they pay a handsome sum, the money is secondary compared to the prize it produced.

AVAILABILITY OF A PRODUCT IS A KEY TO SUCCESS IN A MARKET

The above example shows that distribution is an important strategic element of the marketing mix. The focus of distribution goes way beyond the common misperception that distribution is only logistics. For example, a company can adapt their distribution strategy through the intensity of its distribution channel coverage. In exclusive distribution, the company by choice limits the number of wholesalers and/or retailers it uses in an area. This creates an image of exclusivity in that the customer has to make an effort to obtain the product. An example would be Godiva's tactic to limit the number of stores to exclusive areas and to high-quality locations. It would be difficult for Godiva to create a quality image if they were available at each and every corner candy store.

Selective distribution involves a moderate number of wholesalers and/or retailers. Here an attempt is made to combine good channel control with reasonable profits and sales. In intensive distribution, the goal is to have widespread market coverage. Such a strategy is particularly appropriate for less expensive items in which impulse purchases occur often. The goal is to place the product in front of the consumer so that a purchase is made.

TYPES OF DISTRIBUTION CHANNELS

There are basically two different types of distribution channels: direct and indirect.

A direct distribution channel involves no intermediaries and is used by companies that wish to control its entire marketing program from production to purchase. It is an appropriate strategy when the firm wishes to have close contact with the consumer and when the target market is focused. Often it makes no sense for a company to involve itself in direct distribution because it involves skills in many areas, such as wholesaling and retailing. The example of the tape shop (which sold only different types of tape and no paper) in an old episode of *Saturday Night Live* illustrated how ill-advised such a strategy could be.

An indirect channel of distribution involves intermediaries between the producer and consumer, such as wholesalers, jobbers and retailers. Such a strategy is appropriate for firms that wish to increase their market reach, give up distribution functions, and accept that they are relinquishing channel control. In many foreign countries such as the PRC and Japan, the number of intermediaries are mindboggling.

KEY 21

How to effectively integrate the 4 P's of marketing

By now it should be obvious that marketing strategy involving the 4 P's cannot be developed independent of the target market and the target market cannot be chosen without an in-depth focus on the 4 P's.

LAS VEGAS, THE NEXT THEME

On my last trip to Las Vegas in the winter, I noticed a lot of building activity and new casinos. Mandalay Bay had just opened, as did Bellagio; Venice was opening and Paris Vegas was due to open in the Fall. Vegas already boasted Luxor; New York, New York; Mirage; Treasure Island; Circus Circus; and Excalibur. As a marketer, it was apparent that a new and different theme for a casino might have a significant impact on a company's bottom line. But what should be that theme? Here marketing research is extremely important. Frequent visitors to Las Vegas could be queried and asked questions about what themed casino that does not currently exist would be attractive to them? More abstractly, they could be asked about when and where did they spend the most exciting vacation of their life.

The identification of a theme would begin to address the product issues. For example, it might be that a Viking theme turned out to be the best candidate. The question then becomes how to operationalize such a theme in a casino context. Pricing issues could be covered in terms of room and food rates, whereas placement issues might

The meek have to inherit the earth — they sure don't know how to market it.

Jeno Paulucci, **New York Times**

be linked to the physical location of the structure. In terms of promotion, because there are few Vikings left in America (except in Minnesota), one would have to begin thinking about broadening the target market. Is the Viking resort and casino to be a family resort? (like Excaliber); is it to be extremely up-scale? (like Bellagio) or is it to be a place for young affluent couples (like Venice). This, of course, gets into target market issues, and clearly the 4 P's of marketing cannot be effectively developed without a consideration of the target market.

SMALL MISTAKES CAN BE LARGE WHEN INTEGRATING THE 4 P'S INTO A CONSISTENT WHOLE

Small details can often have a big impact on the integration of the marketing strategy elements of the 4 P's and the target market. For example, if Bellagio is so up-scale, then how come there are nickel slot machines? Why isn't there a kosher deli in the New York, New York casino? Wouldn't this be a natural? The kosher deli happens to be in Luxor, which is based on an Egyptian theme. I asked the manager of the deli how many Pastrami sandwiches did the Jews eat when they were slaves in Egypt in the time of Moses? The real question, of course, is what is a kosher deli doing in Egypt? His response, that "it's ethnic," does not cut the mustard! The bottom line is that when you come up with a marketing strategy for your product, focus hard and long on the consistency between the 4 P's and the target market. A consistent strategy is an effective strategy.

International marketing as a potential focus of the company

The decision to "go international" is not necessarily a simple one, and may not be successful if a company simply transforms a marketing program that works in the United States to a foreign country. Consider the Chevy Nova. One does not have to go much beyond the name of the car to predict that it would not be a success in countries such as Mexico, Spain and France. In these countries the translation of the car's name is "car that does not go." So what issues should a company consider when it wants to enter a foreign market?

STRATEGIC CONSIDERATIONS BEFORE ENTERING A FOREIGN MARKET

The firm should consider the international marketing environment just as it would the domestic marketing environment if a product were to be introduced domestically. The international marketing environment, however, is a bit more sophisticated than the domestic marketing environment. This is because issues related to international trade come to the forefront. What trade restrictions would the company face? Restrictions such as tariffs and quotas can add significant costs or even limit the flexibility of a well-planned marketing strategy.

Beyond trade restrictions, consideration should be given to a country's economic environment. That is, what is the country's industrial structure and income distribution? As Kotler and Armstrong (1991, p. 578) note, "the country's industrial structure shapes its product and service needs, income levels, and employment levels."

If a country has few people who make money over the poverty level, it may be ineffective to attempt to sell certain products there. For example, a firm that makes film producing equipment may feel that its market is slowly dying in the United States as we switch to digital. At issue is whether this company could enter another country such as Mexico. However, if the country has only a small percentage of people who live above the poverty level, then film development may be perceived to be a luxury item. Hence, market entry into Mexico should be reconsidered.

Other factors that are part of a country's marketing environment include a consideration of the political-legal environment. This includes a consideration of the country's attitude toward foreign goods, issues related to political stability, government bureaucracy and monetary regulations. For example, bribes are a large part of cutting through the political and legal red-tape in many countries in the third-world. An American company entering such a market would have little experience with such protocols and may fail despite a well-planned marketing strategy.

Finally, the cultural environment is a key factor to study. A friend of my father once had the idea that certain African countries were under-served by movie theaters. He spent a considerable amount of money by building movie theaters and playing first-run movies seen in America. In one particular country, not one person came to the theater, even after weeks had passed and many different movies were screened. Further investigation revealed that in this particular country, men and women could not be seen in public together. When a partition was placed in the theater separating men and women, the theaters were a big hit!

WHAT IS THE BEST WAY TO ENTER A FOREIGN MARKET?

The easiest way to enter a foreign market is by exporting. A second way is through some a joint venture that includes licensing or contract manufacturing or management contracting. For example, Hilton Hotels often entered foreign markets by obtaining an interest in foreign hotels in return for the Hilton name and the provision of management expertise.

Finally, another option would be direct investment typically through developing foreign-based assembly or manufacturing plants. The advantages could be the avoidance of certain taxes and tariffs, and the availability of cheaper labor. Costs of this strategy might be reflected in inferior product quality and exposure to certain risks, such as currency devaluation and or government intervention.

Case Study:
A marketing success story

Oops! My beautiful etched-glass doorknob just fell and broke on my tile floor. Where am I going to get a replacement? After calling eight or nine local hardware stores, I finally came across one that carries etched-glass door handles and much, much more. Restoration Hardware is the company's name and aside from carrying beautiful door knobs, the chain offers upscale home furnishings, bath items, cleaning supplies as well as hard-to-find interior building and decorative materials. The chief executive is Stephen Gorden, and his idea for the company started about 20 years ago when he took up a project to restore an old Victorian mansion in Eureka, California. He noticed that few stores carried the material he needed to restore the house back to its 1900's splendor.

Today, the chain has 65 locations throughout the United States and British Columbia. Plans are to add about 25–30 more stores each year into the near future. Revenues have increased from $4.2

million in 1994 to about $200 million today, almost a 50-fold increase in revenues in a scant five years. On the face of it, the chain appears to be extremely successful. According to Gordon, the store has a unique image and a clearly defined customer base (Massingil 1999):

> "Our customer is dead center among the baby boomers, as I am. We've always had a buying strategy of trying to ascertain what the customer wants. Really, we're just buying what we like and assuming that there are enough people like us who concur. It's not really a strategic process."

As a marketer, a quick analysis of Restoration shows some of the key elements of success. A clearly defined customer base (baby boomers who value nostalgia) linked with products that are of interest to the customer. The company has also carved out an interesting niche in the hardware market, that of nostalgic upscale products.

However, there are also elements of concern that must be addressed in any critical marketing review. First, is the increase in sales totally accountable by the increase in the number of outlets? That is, how are same-store sales doing over the same time period? They could be decreasing, yet revenues would increase because of a dramatic increase in store locations. Second, one must take into account the competition, such as Pier 1 imports, Cost-Plus, Crate & Barrel, Bed Bath and Beyond and Pottery Barn. If they attack Restoration Hardware by offering some of the same or similar products, is Restoration uniquely positioned in the mind of the consumer to defend itself? Third, Mr. Gordon's statement should send out warnings to any strategic marketer. To claim that his buying process is not necessarily strategic and is based upon "buying what we like and assuming that there are enough people like us who concur," is counter to the marketing research process and outright dangerous if "what we like" is no longer what the target customer is interested in buying.

Finally, Restoration's success is linked to a continued interest by the target market in the type of product that is offered by Restoration. This must be monitored on a continual basis to insure Restoration's continued success.

Case Study:
A marketing challenge

You are near the top of Mount Everest and you don't feel the cold. No, you're not dead! You're wearing North Face clothing inside of a North Face tent. This company has established itself as the premier high-end/high-priced equipment and apparel brand for the serious outdoors-person in the $5 billion specialty outdoor market. To continue its high growth, the company wants to stretch its line into the broader $30 billion casual sportswear market. Its first move in this direction was a $10 million purchase of boot maker La Sportiva. Consumer behavior trends show that the outdoor look has become hot with the Range Rover/cellular phone crowd and there is a significant change in lifestyle towards outdoor leisure.

Although it would seem that the company could easily move downstream from serious to casual outdoor wear, such a decision would not come without potential problems. The first issue is whether the introduction of casual wear would negatively affect the quality image of North Face. Right now, North Face is perceived as the "Cadillac" of outdoor wear by the serious out-doors-person. If they begin to produce less expensive casual wear, would this cheapen their image? If so, this may cause North Face to do an about face with sales quickly heading south. To enter into the casual wear market, North Face plans to increase distribution, from the current 1,500 specialty stores to another 2,500 general retailers, such as Nordstrom and Footlocker. At issue is whether to carry both the serious and causal line at the same outlets.

Even more of a concern is the issue of branding. Here, many concerns come up. First, should the casual line carry the North Face name and, if it does, would it cannibalize the original line by taking sales away from it? Second, if both lines carry the North Face name, how would this impact the overall North Face image? Many current retailers are concerned that if North Face expands into other retail shops, discounting might occur, which would affect their ability to sell the product. Finally, in terms of promotion, if North face is to introduce two different lines, would it make sense to advertise both together or to maintain their current image, develop a specific promotional objective for each line that is non-overlapping?

This discussion shows that even a marketing decision that seems simple involves many other complex strategic decisions that the company must make that are interrelated. No change in marketing strategy is easy to make, and it takes in-depth marketing analysis to outline an appropriate strategy.

Future directions of marketing strategies

I n this Key I will peer into my crystal ball in an attempt to outline three trends that I believe will become evident as we enter the next millenium. Close attention to such trends combined with marketing action may help to make a company more competitive in the year 2000 and beyond.

CONSUMER SATISFACTION WILL INCREASE IN IMPORTANCE
As markets become more and more competitive, companies will continue to search for ways to differentiate themselves from competitors. These distinctions could be based on one of the 4 P's, such as product differences, advertising differences, distribution or price. However, companies will come to the realization that ultimately it is the consumer's satisfaction with the service experience that can make a key difference in motivating product purchase. Customer satisfaction leads to repeat purchase, which can ultimately lead to gains in market share. For example, I recently completed a study designed to examine the

**Strategy and timing are
the Himalayas of marketing.
Everything else is the Catskills.**

Al Ries and Jack Trout, **Marketing Warfare**

drivers of patient satisfaction with doctors of an H.M.O. Not surprisingly, the key driver of patient satisfaction was the doctor's manner with the patient and whether the doctor had a sense of humor. In an area in which it is difficult for the novice to evaluate the quality of care, other factors linked to the service encounter may surprisingly come to the forefront.

The company of the future must pay closer attention to the way in which the consumer is treated. One of Nordstrom's keys to success is the personal attention given to each customer as he/she shops in the store. Can this be said of Kmart? An attention to service quality sometimes must be scripted into the way a company describes its consumers. For example, my bank, First Federal, does not have customers, it has clients. Disney does not deal with a crowd, they cater to their guests. The way you describe your clientele affects the way you interact with them.

I recently had a horrible experience at an unnamed bank, attempting to refinance my home loan. This bank prides itself in delivering customer service and satisfaction with the saying: "You're not alone at Fourth American (fictitious name)." I mailed them a letter stating that alone was misspelled, it should be a loan! Don't let this happen to your company.

ADVERTISING WILL CONTINUE TO FIND ALTERED FORMS IN A MORE CLUTTERED ENVIRONMENT

Twenty years ago, Trout and Ries (1979) reported that:

> "With only 5 percent of the world's population, America consumes 57 percent of the world's advertising output. The per capita consumption of advertising in the U.S. today is about $200 per year. If you spend $1,000,000 a year on advertising, you are bombarding the average consumer with less than 1/2 cent of advertising spread out over 365 days—a consumer who is already exposed to $200 worth of advertising from other companies."

This data was from 20 years ago, so imagine the numbers today. With so much competition for the consumer's attention, advertising must be much more attention-getting to have an impact. As noted in Key 18, advertising has appeared in the form of product placement and has sprouted on the Web within the past 10 years. Where will it appear next, and more importantly, what can you do to make your target market attend to it? I predict a significant increase in the use of celebrities in advertising (see Key 8) because celebrities tend to increase the attention paid to an ad.

Also on the rise might be other creative forms of advertising. For example, in Israel recently a society for the prevention of breast cancer came up with an ad in a medical journal that asked the reader (typically a doctor) to look at a woman's breast in the ad and note if anything was wrong. They were then asked to hold it up to the light. The use of a watermarked paper revealed the beginning of breast cancer and got the doctor's attention. The headline was, "Sometimes what you do not see at first can become very dangerous later." Ads that place the viewer "in the action" may also become the fashion with the use of interactive media on the Web. Absolute Vodka already has an Absolut museum on the Web, where people can simulate walking through galleries viewing a literal museum of Absolut ads.

MARKETING ACTIVITIES WILL DRAMATICALLY INCREASE ON THE WEB

The beginning of this phenomenon is already happening. Companies such as E-Bay, Ubid, Yahoo, and Amazon.com all offer auction services making the entire world a big swap meet. This past April, E-Bay reported profits of $5.9 million and revenues of $34 million for the first quarter alone. The company hosted 22.9 million auctions, an increase of more than 68 percent over the previous quarter. This suggests that consumers who use auctions should consider learning bidding skills, a relatively narrowly utilized art. It seems possible that in the near future we will have the capacity to purchase everything from airline tickets to home loans over the Web. This will have a significant impact on in-person retailing as we know it today. Moreover, the company who can determine what attributes are important to their target market when purchasing over the Web will have an advantage. The idea of "good service" may be translated into a secure purchase and quick delivery time.

The Web may also redefine the traditional approach we use to purchase. For example, Priceline.com allows the consumer to specify a price for a product which is either accepted or rejected by the company. Competitors, attack this approach by calling it a game and by segmenting to those consumers who are used to the more traditional approach in which the retailer (not the consumer), names the price.

The lesson of this book is that like the physical world, the world of marketing is in a constant state of flux. Those companies who stand pat with a once successful marketing plan are those most likely to fall flat in the not-so-distant future. Probably the greatest lesson here is to constantly monitor your marketing strategy and to change when change is needed. Be creative, "think out of the box." Like Ted Levitt (1960) suggests, do not hesitate to come up with questions and ideas that make your current product obsolete. Better your company should think of these issues than the competitor. Hopefully you will have the answers.

For example, a young marketer recently suggested that Long Beach's Aquarium of the Pacific should let kids "sponsor" fish. For five dollars a year, the sponsoring child gets his picture and that of his fish on a sponsorship card. According to the young marketer, this would accomplish three objectives: 1. the Aquarium would have a new source of revenue at virtually no cost; 2. attendance would increase as kids came back time and again to see their fish; and, 3. children would learn to care about the environment by caring about their fish. What makes this idea particularly interesting is that it came from my 9 1/2 year old son! Great ideas can come from everywhere and everyone!

REFERENCES

Alpert, Frank H., and Michael A. Kamins. (1994), "Pioneer Brand Advantage and Consumer Behavior: A Conceptual Framework and Propositional Inventory," *Journal of the Academy of Marketing Science*, 22 (Summer), pp. 244–253.

Alpert, Frank H., and Michael A. Kamins (1995), "An Empirical Investigation of Consumer Memory, Attitude and Perceptions Toward Pioneer and Follower Brands," *Journal of Marketing*, 59 (October), pp. 34–45.

Andreason, Alan R. (1985), "'Backward' Marketing Research," *Harvard Business Review*, 63 (May–June), pp. 176–182.

Borden, Neil H. (1964), "The Concept of the Marketing Mix," *Journal of Advertising Research*, 4 (June), pp. 2–7.

Bourne, Francis S. (1957), "Group Influence in Marketing and Public Relations," in Rensis Likert and Samuel P. Hayes, Jr., Eds., *Some Applications of Behavioral Research* (Paris: UNESCO).

Carpenter, Gregory and Kent Nakamoto (1989), "Consumer Preference Formation and Pioneering Advantage," *Journal of Marketing Research*, 26 (August), pp. 285–298.

Goldenberg, Jacob, David Mazursky and Sorin Solomon (1999), "Toward Identifying the Inventive Templates of New Products: A Channeled Ideation Approach," *Journal of Marketing Research,* 36 (May), pp. 200–210.

Golder, Peter and Gerard Tellis (1993), "Pioneer Advantage: Marketing Logic or Marketing Legend," *Journal of Marketing Research,* 30 (May), pp. 158–170.

Kamins, Michael A., and Henry Assael (1993), "Two-sided versus One-sided Appeals: a Cognative Perspective on the Effect of Trial Upon Belief Change," *Journal of Marketing Research,* 24 (February), pp. 29–39.

Kamins, Michael A., and Kamal Gupta (1994), "Congruence Between Spokesperson and Product Type: A Matchup Hypothesis Perspective," *Psychology and Marketing,* 11 (6), pp. 569–588.

Kardes, Frank and Gurumurthy Kalyanaram (1992), "Order-Of-Entry Effects on Consumer Memory and Judgment: An Information Integration Perspective," *Journal of Marketing Research,* 29 (August), pp. 343–357.

Kinnear, Thomas C., and James R. Taylor (1991), *Marketing Research,* Fourth Edition. McGraw-Hill Publishing Company New York, New York.

Kotler, Philip (1994), *Marketing Management,* Eighth Edition. Prentice-Hall, Englewood Cliffs, New Jersey.

Kotler, Philip and Gary Armstrong (1991), *Principles of Marketing,* Fifth Edition. Prentice-Hall, Englewood Cliffs, New Jersey.

Lavidge, Robert J., and Gary A. Steiner (1961), "A Model for Predictive Measurements of Advertising Effectiveness," *Journal of Marketing*, 25 (October), pp. 59–62.

Levitt, Theodore (1960), "Marketing Myopia." *Harvard Business Review*, 38 (July-August), pp. 45–56.

Massingil, Teena (1999) "The Rise of Restoration Hardware," *Daily News*, 88 (114), p. 1 Business Section (April 24).

Ries, Al and Jack Trout (1993), *The 22 Immutable Laws of Marketing*. HarperCollins Publishers, New York, New York.

Sirgy, M. Joseph (1982), "Self-Concept in Consumer Behavior: A Critical Review." *Journal of Consumer Research,* 9 (December), pp. 287–300.

Trout, Jack and Al Ries (1979), "The Positioning Era: A View Ten Years Later," *Advertising Age*, 50, July 16.

INDEX

AUTHOR

MICHAEL A. KAMINS, Ph.D., is an Associate Professor of Marketing at the Marshall School of Business Administration at the University of Southern California. He has taught at both the undergraduate and graduate levels at USC for over 15 years. Dr. Kamins has published over 30 articles in journals including the *Journal of Marketing Research*, *Journal of Advertising Research*, and *Journal of Consumer Psychology*. Additionally, he has consulted for such firms as AT&T, Breath Assure, Canon, Hilton, MGM, Sony Tristar, and Thompson and Vons Companies.